LIMINAL

POEMS BY

DOUGLAS REID SKINNER

UHLANGA

2017

Published in Cape Town, South Africa by uHlanga in 2017

UHLANGAPRESS.CO.ZA

Distributed outside South Africa by the African Books Collective

AFRICANBOOKSCOLLECTIVE.COM

ISBN: 978-0-620-76256-4

Edited by Nick Mulgrew

Cover design by Nick Mulgrew
Cover image based on a drawing by Cleone Cull

The body text of this book is set in Garamond Premier Pro 11PT on 15PT

※

Some of the poems in this collection were first published in the following journals
and publications: *Carapace*, *New Contrast*, *The McGregor Poetry Festival
Anthology 2015*, *Stanzas*, and *Africa Alive!* (African Sun Press, 2015).

*The publication of this book has in part
been made possible by the generosity of
David Cheyne*

CONTENTS

...the shimmer
of matter we inhabit for a while
WILLIAM MATTHEWS

...the sky flashes, the great sea yearns,
we ourselves flash and yearn
JOHN BERRYMAN

In the Library

Why do we keep anything?
All morning I hear the pages
rustling softly in the stacks.
Autumn comes to all leaves.

This Infinitesimal Fraction of Being

I – PAST TENSE

Which is the life you'd rather have lived,
whose body's the one you'd rather have been?
What paths of destiny and bright trouvailles
would you have rather seen?

Such questions torture right to the end –
the conjectures, the dreams, the imagining.
But without them you never get past the beginning
and into the rushing, whelming stream

that comes, from nowhere, to make you sing.

II – FUTURE TENSE

When you see, while strolling hand-in-hand
on the sunny side of Motcomb Street,
a Buddleia growing from the side of a house
with all of its soil but a handful of grit,

you know that over us will rise
an effortless veil, as we steadily go
down and into the crowded barrow
of species that have been discarded

for those better fitting the world ahead –
the world we will not know.

A Letter to Dante Alighieri and Robert Frost

– i.m. Patrick Cullinan (1933–2011)

It remains unclear as to whether or not
there's any way out of the forest;
which is why, I suppose, that whenever
I encounter others among the trees,
they always seem as lost as me.

Some are old, yet seem so young;
some are young, yet wear their years
as if they carried all the world.
Some say that wandering's all they've known;
for some, their wandering's just begun.

Each time I find a path, I hope
for fields that slope towards a beach,
a sea that ends in clouds and sky,
the promise of an open reach,
a sense of place and time and ease.

And yet the trail keeps going cold,
it leads to where I've crossed before.
Where each path ends, another begins,
and all that's left to us it seems
is going on from where we've been.

WRITING

We never quite knew
what we wished to describe –
a kind of countryside
we thought we understood

but had never been to,
imagining that if only
we could get there, could
reach that place, if only

we could return to where
we'd never been, the place
for which we'd longed,
the place we had desired

for the longest time,
and if only we could
inhabit that house,
walk on those fields,

the ones filled with flowers,
with all the scents
we thought we could recognise,
that we could remember,

but for which the words
would always elude...
and it's true, there were times
when we felt elevated,

balancing high
on the ancient ridge
of eroding rocks and boulders,
the wind whipping

leaves and twigs all around,
times when we believed
we'd arrived at
exactly that place,

the one that we never knew
until we were there,
until we had found
ourselves in the place

to which we'd always
been heading
without knowing where,
without chart or review,

the one we had always known
but had never been to...

SURROUNDED BY MOUNTAINS

– for Gus Ferguson, Franschhoek, 2014

A plume of smoke is rising into cloud.
The cloud descends below the forest line.
The trees are ghosts of shadows and lost light.

The light fades fast until you cannot see
beyond the angled roofs across the town.
The windows of a house flare into flame

as one last flash of sunlight from the pass
leads you to the thought of what's beyond:
long, deep valleys carved by untold time.

You had a destination once, but now
that's lost beneath the weight of leaves.
Instead, you wait alone and watch for clues

to what gives all the light and clouds and trees,
the smoke and flying range of saw-tooth peaks,
meanings that will hold against the storm

the coming of which you've seen the early signs.
A plume of smoke is rising into cloud.
A slight wind whirls it round and round and round.

WINDING TUNNELS

The road to Port Alfred unwraps and winds
up over hills that rise to the south of town.
Long stretches are marred by bumps and cracks,
a patchwork of repairs now always in need
of the kind of attention it will never receive.

Once on the ridge, sweeping views reveal
receding valleys and slopes, each one greyer
than the one in front, each bend bringing
memories to relish from a childhood recalled.
(Or at least one you imagine must have been.)

Then, the slow slope down to the cooler coast
and a sudden descent to the languid Kowie.
Still there, as you enter the town, the same shop
that sold fish and chips on Sunday evenings
as we'd leave, curled up on the back seat, sharing

a warm portion sprinkled with salt and vinegar
before licking our fingers and falling asleep
to the bass rhythm of a neighbour's V8, carrying
us back through winding tunnels of light
to the more uncertain shades of home.

In Perspective

I must have asked Robert's daughter to stand
just inside the frame with a shovel in her hand
because a photographer once taught me to make
sure that the viewer has a sense of size and space,

so that everything you see is in perspective
when looking at, for instance, this interior in '86
of Doug's rickety farm shed in the humpback hills
to the southwest, not far from Grahamstown.

The cows are in for milking, waiting patiently
in the stalls for each in turn to be tickled
by soft hands and unburdened while standing
without fussing, getting on with their chewing,

flicking ears and casually swishing their tails
from side to side to chase away incessant flies.
The dog's curled in a corner and fast asleep.
A cat watches from the side and hopes for a lid.

The light floods in through clouded windows,
edging Lorna's hair with a halo of gold coin;
it seems almost solid, made tangible by a fine
gossamer of dust hanging in the breathless air.

Doug died of a cough and the farm was sold.
Lorna grew up and was tickled in turn.
Robert settled down to afternoons on a balcony,
drinking tea and watching weather on the Bay.

But the cows, oh, the cows, when I close my eyes tight,
are still in their stalls, washed over by light,
patiently standing, with ears and tails twitching,
patiently waiting to be tickled and eased.

Out of a Summer Night May Come

When you've watched over someone
for the whole of their life,
you might be excused for thinking
you know them.
But you don't.

The boy in the photograph
running with freedom across the lawn
to throw himself
into the arms of his mother
with fullest abandon

as she bends to meet him
soon becomes a man
filled with his own
uncertainties and dreams,
joy and desolation.

And as you see it all grow and grow
to make a whole person,
so you come to know
less and less of exactly who is
behind the look, inside the laughter

when he comes in through
the front door and out
of a warm summer night
to embrace her again,
as if he were still

the same boy made of India rubber,
not yet knowing
that a day will come
when he'll cradle her in his arms
as her breathing fades to shallow.

But for now, in this
one and only now
in which we actually are –
in this infinitesimal fraction of being –
he is still that boy

seen running across the photograph
pondered long by a man
before he looks away
and into the distance
beyond the shadowy garden.

The Pain Is Sweet

– after Cortázar

I touch your mouth with my fingers,
and trace the outline as if I am drawing
your lips with my hand, as if your
mouth is parting for the very first time.

All I need do is close my eyes
to undo it all, to start over and create
a new mouth, the one that I desire,
that my hand wants and sketches

on your face, this mouth I have
elected from all possible mouths,
chosen to trace across your face,
the one that by some strange quirk of fate

precisely coincides with the mouth
I see smiling up at me from below.
You look intently at me, closing
the distance between us, our eyes

growing larger and larger as they
suddenly overlap and then disappear
into each other, our breathing confused,
our mouths engaged in a tender sparring,

our tongues delicately reaching
into corners where a silent, freighted air
comes and goes with its familiar perfumes.
Then I run my fingers through your hair,

slowly caress your hair as we meld,
our mouths filled to overflowing
with the lingering fragrance of flowers,
the quick, intense movements of fish.

And if we bite, the pain is sweet;
and if we drown in a brief, overwhelming
gasping together for the sanction of air,
the moment of death will be beautiful.

Then, at last, there is only one water,
one heady flavour of ripened fruits,
and I feel you trembling gently against me,
like the moon in a rippling stream.

BOTTLES OF SCENT

Because the forgotten
outweighs the remembered
as an ocean a pond,

the fleeting, the shadowed,
the velleities that limn
and almost correspond

to what was once hymn
or haunting day long,
ineffable, yet possible,

you suddenly wake
in the half-light of dawn
to a rise-and-fall song

that engenders recall
of hands that you held,
bottles of scent,

a dress with blue flowers,
the chair near the door,
a cup of weak coffee,

the voice that could call
through window and wall,
the voice that could salve

the wounds and the gall.

Ludwig's Last Letter

The challenge was always (though
not always understood to be so)
to devise an exact way of thinking

that could constitute a coherent body
of thought. Neglect the way
and the body shrivels, he knew.

Focus on the body, and you lose
your way. After so many years,
he concluded with a sigh, he was

no closer to finding that unblemished,
straight road able to deliver him
into the parish of a future where,

behind low hills, he would finally find –
complete with thatched-roof cottages,
a Post Office and greengrocer,

tea rooms, an old stone church
and a busy public house on the green –
a village of thought on a summer's day,

with ordinary ideas sitting quietly
in the square, or leisurely walking
along its paved diagonals, going

steadily about their business.

Equilibrium

– to Nick

Writing all day can ruin a shoulder
if you're not careful. All that leaning
on one limb as spring moves the blood
awful deep, making you rise early again
to take step after step across the void
on the old, uncertain, knotted string
you keep meaning to mend, despite
never having figured out how
you might do it – at least not yet.

~

The morning choirs of feathered gangs
yell at one another much like the no-
longer-boys, not-quite-men, who
muck about on a street corner with
a palpable air of intent. Though, this time,
nothing comes by to disturb their
unbalanced equilibrium. The birds
are a distraction – anything is – and yet
without them, how empty the garden.

~

The Chinese sage got it right,
who, writing late into the night,
smiled and said that you only begin
to understand tea after the fifth cup.
It's the same with books, I guess, though
that flimsiest of things, a page, can quickly
unman (or unwoman) the pilot flying
high above the patterns of fields and hills
when the engine coughs and suddenly stalls.

~

Skeleton and muscles, sinews and organs,
each neatly in its place. The intent eyes
scanning the room, the ears cocked, feet
steadily tapping out a rhythm. Press too hard
with a pen, he knew, and it all adjusts;
and in adjusting, deforms; and in deforming,
sends messages through delicate wires
to the lonely, hunched-over ghost who has,
once again, to abandon his unruffled pose.

~

The late nights have yet to grow warm.
A heavy dewfall coats branches, leaves and lawn
where some nocturnal mammal has left
footprints... But wait! That was me, looking
for... it was me, looking for... Surely this
forced march has to lead to somewhere?
Back to where it all began? Exactly.
Circumambulating the mulberry bush.
Be careful. Writing can ruin a shoulder.

(It keeps you fit, but for what I cannot say.)

GUNSHOTS ECHOED

Joining the local club, as daily urged,
meant putting on their uniform.
It also meant respecting codes
not always quite the same as yours.

In such dilemmas we seem to see
the lines of fault that inevitably
define the nature of our being.
Each day I chose instead to be

alone and walk for hours across
the land, until an afternoon
when gunshots echoed out from trees
close to where I was to pass.

Perhaps some hunters busy there
were flushing birds or stalking deer,
although, because I could not see,
because the path I always took

led up and over sunlit hills
of ripened wheat, tomorrow's food,
I never knew exactly what
or who was busy in that wood.

THE SENTENCE

So, at last you embrace the rules –
or, at least, an idea of them – and set
out to sea, taking oars, a furled sail
and a box of rations to last a week.

You stow water in old wine bottles.
A compass would have been a wise choice,
but who has such wisdom
at the beginning?

Who plans for landfall, a long beach
with waves the height of your knees
that seem to cheer your arrival
before falling at your feet?

The weather keeps shifting,
promising this, delivering that.
The caulking slowly shrinks.
You notice beads of wet at your feet.

What to do, how to stay dry?
A baling bucket would have been ideal,
but who is that thoughtful
when setting out?

From time to time you spot trees
waving on the horizon.
How to steer towards them?
A rudder would mean

that you'd planned for your arrival,
had an inkling of what would be required,
had foreseen the sound of the keel
sighing up the sand and suddenly halting,

and you stepping over the gunwales at last
and onto a raised pebble beach –
a whole country beyond it –
alert to the treeline, pen in hand.

Coffee and a Pastry

– Venice, 1995

1   The slap of olive water
echoes in shadows
below slate-blue arches.
Winter's not quite done;
spring flatters to deceive
and sulks in the wings.
Wind and tide
have flooded the alleys
where everyone steps
gingerly along
improvised walkways,
not wanting to wet
their well-heeled feet.
A persistent drizzle
falls all morning,
discomfiting tourists
who brush without feeling
past one another.
You can almost see
the buildings settling,
inch by inch,
into the centuries.

11   Paola's laugh is infectious.
     Over coffee and a pastry
     she recounts a life
     of watching from
     high windows perched
     above the water's
     changing face.
     How, after all the years
     of writing about
     the moods reflected
     on narrow canals,
     the late-afternoon light
     breaking through clouds
     and washing across
     the old brick buildings
     propped on sticks,
     she is leaving behind
     the swishing of oars,
     the rise and fall
     of the *vaporetti*.
     Nothing gets done,
     she says with a sigh.
     Politicians squabble,
     the city drowns.

Getting Lost

– for Marco

On a grey day at the fag end of March,
with pewter-flat water through windows
to the left and right, and distant boats
ploughing steadily through the brine,

the Vicenza-Venice train (2nd Class)
is overheated. Slumped in their seats,
with bleary, sleep-short eyes and the lingering
aroma of cigarette smoke hurriedly

inhaled just before boarding, students
tap, heads down, on hand-held devices.
Everyone sways gently in childhood
as the old carriages barrel noisily into

an endlessly receding vanishing point.
"Sasha didn't phone me. I hope she
managed to find the hotel," worries Marco,
burdened by the weight of being a sheep dog,

gravity dragging irresistibly at his
up-until-one-translating-her-poem eyelids.
"Oh, I wouldn't worry," replies Douglas.
"She's clearly not afraid of getting lost.

"And it's that sort of city: walk in a circle,
look at the map; circle, map, circle
and map; you soon find your way.
The only bother, really, is the water."

Twenty Years On

– Venice, 2015

> *...in the dawn, the mist,*
> *in that dimness*

I   Utter stillness, empty air, before boats
slice the surface, wake after wake, with
echoing engines and curling waves
that run to old, crusted walls;
before the markets, before the stalls,
before the caffé owners open their doors
for the early birds.

II   A Tang artisan would stare hard at such water,
his hands tingling, wanting to carve
the green stone, his arthritic fingers feeling
for the lines of a dragon-handled
cup of such perfection it would seem
to the Emperor as if he were holding
the tea itself, and nothing else.

III   A slight fall in temperature marks the presence
of Locanda Montin's doorway shades
still longing for the years
when they could sing and hold court,
in love with the sound of words
and imploring passers-by to pause,
raise a glass, and remember poetry's cause.

IV   Noon bells echo across the canals.
      Unfamiliar words in the reading room
      mingle and mell, shake hands, embrace and kiss,
      slide together, run long fingers
      over the audience, look to escape
      through window or door, before
      ending in a pile left lying on the floor.

V   In restaurants and squares,
      the evening crowds lean back in chairs,
      laugh and chatter, eat and natter,
      and empty their glasses
      before the mist brings forth an echoing walk
      past crumbling walls and, below a bridge,
      obsidian water that reflects, distorts.

LEISURELY CLOUDS

There is only now, and only here.
Where else could we be?
When else might we live?

The crowd is boisterous,
arms and legs jostle,
there are flags, excited voices,

horses, dogs barking
with untethered excitement.
The clowns will soon arrive.

Words shuffle through the crowd,
a lone balloon floats away.
Musicians on the bandstand

dressed to the nines
keep themselves busy
tuning their instruments.

The tables are covered
with baked goods, sweetmeats
and fruit, all sizes of bottle.

Nearby, a small boy leans
over the pond and watches
boatmen sketching ripples.

He is alone and doesn't hear
the noise, remains entranced
by skies below, the leisurely clouds

and high formations of geese
waving steady farewells
across and across blue paper.

GRAVITY

Why make haste towards the period
          waiting at sentence end?
Because I know it's there, he said;
          the ending is my only friend.

Because

Because there were at least three things to think about,
by the time he had reached the landing
nothing remained lodged in his memory.

Having ascended the stairs to do what it was
he had wanted to do, but was not quite able to recall,
he found himself staring blankly at the floor,

trying to remember what he had resolved to do
before tilting forward and beginning to walk,
before standing and leaning enough off vertical

to take the stairs two at a time to the landing
where he now stood, ready to do what he had
wanted to do, prepared but unable to recall

any of the three things, each crowding the others out
and leaving him to look in puzzlement at the door,
at the comical image of a self in the mirror,

at the one who stood wondering who it now was
that was quizzically looking at the one who could know
what it was he had 'to do' (and now looking at you)

before setting out and heading for the next level,
before putting words down, his face in full frown,
his eyes writing on the wall, writing on the floor.

INSTRUCTIONS FOR WRITING A POEM

"Let me dream a small poem," he said to himself.
"Let me write one tonight in a dream while asleep.
I'll need a dream pen and I'll need dream pages,"
he said as he sat on the edge of his bed.

"If I'm lucky," he thought, "this time the dream poem
will arrive as a whole, written out and complete,
and then all that would still be needed of me
is copying it down onto a dream sheet."

So, before he lay down, he decided he had better
write out instructions for the poem as a list.
"Then when I lie sleeping, lost to the world,
dream arm and dream hand will know how it fits."

So he wrote down a list of the lines that he needed,
what words he would use and where they would go,
before lying on his side, curling up in the dark
as the day's old concerns drained out of his head...

and the sheets were covered with falling black snow.

ISLANDS

"If I could only recollect exactly what I wrote
in the dream last night," he thought. "It was
a solution of sorts, even an answer, perhaps."

Part of him had imagined he was sitting on a beach
on an island in the shade of an old fig tree.
It was summer, with a gentle onshore breeze

flicking page corners of a book on his knees.
Looking down, he saw crowds of new words appearing
as if they had all been hidden and waiting

for a hand to glide and reveal them to him,
for a hand to wave and raise them into being.
It was as if all the leaves had floated free,

as if a new language had emerged from the sea,
one for that occasion and for that one only,
each word in the air by its own volition,

each page turning over once it was filled.
"If I could only recall exactly what they were,"
he whispered to himself, "those words that I saw,

"now that I'm ready with a pen and blank page."
But there are no doors into our dreams.
Each mutely drifts along on its own sea.

If You Think You Know How to Write a Poem, Think Again; the Poem Has Other Ideas

She was never home when he knocked on the door,
so he'd walk through the narrow gap in the hedge

and around the back, cupping his hands against the light
and trying to see in. The curtains were always drawn.

He'd hang around, smoke a cigarette, watch birds
fussing in the undergrowth, hoping she would

remain faithful, with eyes for him only. His incantations
never had much effect. She frequently moved elsewhere.

He was never sure of her address, would look for weeks,
in other villages and towns – all along the shore,

in houses in the forests that climbed up mountain slopes.
He could never be quite sure what form she would take,

could have sworn one time it was her, half-hidden
by leaves, sitting on a branch and singing mournfully,

repeating the same phrase over and over, hour after hour.
When a cool onshore wind came off the evening ocean,

he would wait for her touch, for his skin to tighten
and prickle in the air. The moon left him breathless:

it was her face. She could be any one of myriad stars.
So he kept on wandering and knocking, tapping on windows,

whistling to himself with little conviction, even less success.
He never bothered with prayer, or penitence, or scourging,

though a nearby dove intoning the whole repertoire
of melancholy could keep him filled with loyalty

to the invisible, to looking and waiting, day after day,
for the snap of a twig in the shadows, warm breath in his ear.

A Poet

*...there is an old quarrel between
philosophy and poetry...*

offers no solutions,
wrote Tony Hoagland,
just "a lucid diagnosis".
But what can you do
when you're up to the neck
in a host of words
with only the shadow
of a spade to hand?

Two Shirts

– for Michael

In the dream, I'd just emerged from sleep
and wandered, dazed, around the room.
You opened the door and stepped inside,
dressed in clothes for heading to town.

"Ready?" you asked, raising an eyebrow,
but I was groggy, having just woken,
looking down to see what I was wearing.
"Two shirts," I said, smiling ruefully

as I started slowly unbuttoning the one,
thinking out loud, "I must be *ibberbuttle*.
Why on earth do I have two on?"

You grinned and gave a knowing look,
spreading your hands in a weary gesture:
"It's that quaint old faith you have in books."

In The Dream

Again, you are somewhere up ahead, waiting,
and I am here, still in this house, wandering
from room to room, looking to reach you

but getting lost, the road outside changing,
the rooms inside changing, the smiles
of everyone encountered unrecognised.

In the dream, there is only one goal, one
room you wish to find, one room you know
the exact lineaments of, one face you recall

by shape, line and plane, by falling hair,
by the smile that quickly plays in the corners
of averted eyes, the face you recall with clarity,

waiting, somewhere, while you remain
unable to understand whether you're in
the room or you're out of it, or even

what words might describe such dilemmas,
and how this room – the one you might be in,
the place in which you're condemned to wander

from window to window, looking out or in –
how it keeps changing beyond recognition,
keeps on changing, forever, in the dream.

If Not This I, Then Who?

If not this I, then who?
I hear you deeply sigh

as you
cast about for a clue,

wanting to engage,
wishing to assuage

(I hear you cry)
the emptiness of the page.

Prospects

As the story goes, back in the Seventies
an old black prospector walked alone
in mountains up north, every so often
dropping by the Pofadder Hotel
with his worn leather purse
of chipped mineral samples.

The local sergeant looked the other way
as the old guy drank a cold beer
and quietly talked about the latest dolosse
he'd tipped on the bar, poking them
with a wrinkled forefinger and talking
to the knot of men smoking around him.

Hennie Niemand was in the corner
when the old guy strolled in out of the heat
and revealed a handful of dusty chunks
with cone-shaped crystals
he'd found while walking on a farm
forty miles west as the crow flies.

The old guy hadn't come across it before
and wasn't sure what it might be,
but Niemand did. He paid him
for the name and went straight out
and bought the whole concession,
opened a mine and made a small fortune.

The story's probably changed many times
in the telling, but that's pretty much
exactly as McWilliam told it one day
as we drove through the town in a three-tonner,
knackered by a full day's drilling.

"He even built his offices out of it."

Lunch In The Clouds

*"I must now tell you a little about
a Cape expedition..."*

If we'd taken a whole table and legs,
we'd have needed at least three men
to carry it up. But we didn't, and instead
our retainers carried cold meat and wine,
and crockery, cutlery and fine glass.

As we'd been told that we'd find great variety
on the top, Mr Barrow and I slung round
our shoulders tin cases for plants. The path
was reckoned to be about three miles
because of the zigzag way you have to walk.

Not an easy passage, with much scrambling
and a hard slog in unremitting sunlight.
On the way, we found the remains of shoes,
relics that have lain since time immemorial.
Frequent rests were required to recover

from a growing fatigue and heat, and I
rejoiced at the turn of the mountain that
gave us shade and a gully by which we were
to get out on the top after stopping awhile
for spring water mixed with a little port-wine.

After three hours we came out on the height
and relished the sweeping bird's-eye view
of the bays and town below. Then down we sat
to cold meat, our port, Madeira, and Cape wine,
afterwards gathering plants and white pebbles.

Replete, we sang 'God Save the King',
loyal Mr Barrow with his eyes glistening,
after which we packed our things to descend
before night. The only way to get down
was to slip from rock to rock while sitting.

The bets in town had all been on against
my ever reaching the top. Much money
might have been lost. As for me, it is enough
to have the delight of being able to say,
I have seen it laid out, the whole bay,

much as I might have painted it.

FLAGS

– *Debaltseve, Ukraine, 2015*

Now we the victors walk with flags applauding in the breeze,
now we the victors walk with faces wreathed in smiles,
now we who have no weariness or fear can walk and ride
without concern, for we are victors now and here today.

Now we laugh and clap and shout, and stamp our boots
on that old flag the regime flew, on that old flag whose army
left its rooms and holes and trenches dug into the ground,
who left great piles of rubbish, those casings of spent shells,

who left and walked across the fields and down the roads,
who left this place with faces staring blankly at the ground,
who left their lines of footprints in the snow for us to see,
for we are victors now who stamp the earth to make our mark,

for we the victors walk with flags applauding in the breeze,
now we the victors wave our arms and take in all the fields
and hills that once were theirs but now belong to us, for we
have won the prize, the land you see, for now the prize is ours,

for we have won the houses and the streets, for we have won
the churches and the halls, the restaurants and shops are ours,
for we have won the sacred ground where all the dead are held
in time and earth, for we have won the orchards and the trees.

Now we the victors walk with flags applauding in the breeze,
now all the air is ours to breathe, now we can wave our arms
and hold our guns aloft, for they are gone and all you see is ours,
for we are victors now, and now we own the houses and the streets,

and here where yesterday they walked and held their flag aloft
is where we drive our armour through, is where we talk and laugh,
is where we wave and smile and smoke and joke and shout
and point our fingers at our hearts, and say that all is ours,

for we are victors here, Cossack victors here. We are victors now.

ACCOUNTING

The article he was reading
in the Sunday supplement
on the lunacy, malice and suffering
that can plague a society
mentioned figures that had been
totted up of those whose lives
had come to untimely ends
at the hands of regimes
that ruled at the time.

The word 'millions' kept on being
repeated, which reminded him
of a past conversation with a friend
who'd researched such matters.
It concerned the numbers
of those who had been
starved and stabbed in the untilled field
or blown to smithereens;
those shot from a distance,

or raped and beaten
until suicide was the only option;
those poisoned or beheaded
or gassed... he went on,
and had the numbers,
the estimates and the tallies
of the missing, the disappeared,
the erased, at his fingertips.

History is a slaughterhouse,
his friend would say, quoting Singer.
As he read on, he thought,
"But they're just numbers.
A person has a name. Where
are the names? If they'd been
recorded, name after name
in the columns of ledgers
that anyone could read,

that everyone should read
at least once, everyone
running a finger down
page after page in turn
until it becomes unbearable,
impossible not to feel
exactly what it means."
"Where are the names?"
he asked out loud

of no one in particular.

In the Groove

The point of it all depends, he said,
on just what is your point of view.
From a window looking in
or from a chair positioned
on the far side of the room?

Or from above (while standing
on the top of a ladder, e.g.),
or from over the shoulder
of one whose fingers are on the move,
tapping out a lively tune,

the one whose fingers are occupied
assembling the instructions,
a 'how to make' for the thing
that has never been before,
for the thing that is brand new,

the tune that's never been played,
for the window you encounter
with an irresistible view?
Or, closer in, from behind the eyes
of him or her whose point it is

that steadily moves across the field
and leaves a line, leaves a groove,
leaves a puzzling trail of clues?
The point is, he said, as he walked
casually along in well-worn shoes,

the point is to find a way through,
to change all the moves,
change the 'what' and the 'who'
whose which you now consider,
whose where you are going through

until you change the me and the you,
and we, 'the lonely few',
'the good and the true',
explorers with lamps who steadily work
their way down through the gloom,

who carefully play out a thread
they then proceed to lose,
are struck near dumb on arrival,
asking, "What country is...?",
"Where are...?" and, "Who...?"

Smoke Signals

The two animals going at it in the street below
at double decibels, and a car that's idling
as it waits to take a neighbour to the airport

leave him with little alternative except
to abandon all efforts at finding his way
back to the dream landscape across which

he'd been wandering about in the company
of a woman who kept on reappearing
in different guises from behind rocks and trees,

the one who never spoke, who instead waved
her delicate hands, like smoke signals,
explaining something that he couldn't quite

understand, that try as hard as he did
he was never quite able to comprehend,
despite spending whole daytimes puzzling

over the irreducible isolations of being alive
and, notwithstanding mutual murmuring
across pillows, or the cauterising touch

of a finger trailed across valleys and hills
while looking into looking-back eyes,
he wondered whether for once a bright clue

might arise and surprise, enable him to
be inside the other, be inside their where,
gain at last the sense that words exchanged

in the moment might lodge, not disappear,
be stable and consequent, and when recalled
after forty years or more, could readily revive

that when, the when inside, when in the other,
in their body and breathing, in their being alive,
for one impeccable moment their being inside.

EVERY STEP WE TAKE

– for Joan & Johann

At the end, a small music
rising into the rafters,
an hour of drinks and sandwiches,
solemn words and laughter.

The mountain's unperturbed
by all the love and heartbreak,
and all the summits that we reach
summon only heartache.

In truth, we conquer nothing,
are footprints in the melting snow;
petals fading on the path
where once there was a rose.

TEA IN CHINA

– i.m. Alf Wannenburgh (1936–2010)

The best way to eat chestnuts I discovered
one day after stopping for half an hour
under a tree on the upper road to Constantia
that had particularly generous fruit that year.

It was probably because the weather had been
on the mild side during the previous winter,
raining gently for days on end without any
battering storms, followed by an easy spring.

A childhood spent climbing high in the trees
at every opportunity came good as I jungled
about on the branches to shake off fruit,
Peter filling a large box on the car's back seat.

For once, it was calm at Alf's place, the sea
without horses as we pulled up and parked
on Main Road. He cut a cross into the crown
of each nut and set them to roast on a brazier,

moving them carefully with a short stick
as the shells hardened and then quickly peeled
back from the notches, revealing the seed.
We shucked them, added butter and herb salt,

and ate, washing them down with Keemun tea.
Trying over ensuing years to reprise that scene
has always been a waste of time. Smaller fruit,
different trees. And no Alf. And a different sea.

Reflection

Una voragine il tempo
e camminiamo sull'orlo

Subtract yourself, all the way
through substrate to the nub;

the water stills and closes over,
leaving skittish boatmen to

keep skating on reflections,
mimicry in a minor key

of the great and seamless something
that goes on being everything.

LOOKING BACK

Those relatively rich acres of time, days,
turn out to be ephemeral, small spaces
that keep on falling straight out
the backs of our heads,
as if in their passage they shed
not the slightest trace.

Waking in the half-light between seasons,
between night and day, half-formed
shadows resemble what you recollect
when watching a lone blackbird
combing the lawn like a desperate mind
trying to look back.

You know you could record it all
on ivory, smoothed-out pages
with a licked pencil and the quiet engines
of muscle, but that would require
more inattention, not less, because
you'd be busy doing only that

in a fervid sweat, under ramping pressure
to record it all, ad infinitum, unable
to rest, while less and less is seen to happen
and more and more gets written,
nothing in evidence except the steady
scratching of a nib.

And by the time the light has begun
to drain into the landscape's western edge
you would find yourself stranded
with only a fraction done,
a state of panic setting in
and the sound of your heart

battering you into submission.

CLOUDS RISE ON HILLS

Clouds rise on hills to the south.
Is that Poseidon I see in the shapes,
shaggy haired and holding a trident...?

But he's gone before I can tap your arm
and have you look up from the page,
from whatever hidden world you are in.

The train rocks our bodies together,
sunlight streams across the carriage...
and the wind, the wind, keeps making faces,

blowing them away across the day.

The Bottom Line

We are all immortal,
until we aren't.
You can read the writing
and then you can't.

NOTES ON QUOTATIONS

p9   WILLIAM MATTHEWS, *Selected Poems & Translations*
            JOHN BERRYMAN, *77 Dream Songs*

p39   "...in the dawn, the mist,
            in that dimness"
            EZRA POUND, 'Canto XXV'

p51   "...there is an old quarrel between philosophy and poetry..."
            PLATO, *Republic*, 607b5–6

p58   Based on a letter of LADY ANNE BARNARD dated August 10,
            1797, that appeared in *South Africa a Century Ago, Letters
            Written from the Cape of Good Hope (1797–1801)*

p71   "Let us walk on the edge / of Time's abyss"
            TITO BALESTRA, 'untitled', translated by the author from
            the Italian

uHlanga

POETRY FOR THE PEOPLE

— AVAILABLE NOW —

Foundling's Island by P.R. Anderson

White Blight by Athena Farrokhzad, translated by Jennifer Hayashida
IN ASSOCIATION WITH ARGOS BOOKS, USA

Zikr by Saaleha Idrees Bamjee

Milk Fever by Megan Ross

Liminal by Douglas Reid Skinner

Collective Amnesia by Koleka Putuma
CITY PRESS BOOK OF THE YEAR 2017

Thungachi by Francine Simon

Modern Rasputin by Rosa Lyster

Prunings by Helen Moffett
CO-WINNER OF THE 2017 SOUTH AFRICAN
LITERARY AWARD FOR POETRY

Questions for the Sea by Stephen Symons
HONOURABLE MENTION FOR THE
2017 GLENNA LUSCHEI PRIZE FOR AFRICAN POETRY

Failing Maths and My Other Crimes by Thabo Jijana
WINNER OF THE 2016 INGRID JONKER PRIZE FOR POETRY

Matric Rage by Genna Gardini
COMMENDED FOR THE 2016 INGRID JONKER PRIZE FOR POETRY

the myth of this is that we're all in this together by Nick Mulgrew

AVAILABLE FROM GOOD BOOKSTORES IN SOUTH AFRICA
& FROM THE AFRICAN BOOKS COLLECTIVE ELSEWHERE

UHLANGAPRESS.CO.ZA

Printed in the United States
By Bookmasters